NO, GO, AND TELL!

Ms. Clementine's
Personal Safety Lesson

Marilyn A. Pittelli

Illustrated by Rachel Goyeau

PAGE PUBLISHING, INC.
New York, NY

First originally published by Page Publishing, Inc. 2019

ISBN 978-1-64544-572-2 (Paperback)
ISBN 978-1-64584-670-3 (Hardcover)
ISBN 978-1-64544-573-9 (Digital)

Printed in the United States of America

For my grandchildren, with love.

The sun was peeking around the corner of the Lake Avenue School on an early spring morning. As Ms. Clementine drove toward the parking lot, she started to feel excited. She was on her way to Mr. Henry's elementary class to deliver an important safety message.

"Attention!" Mr. Henry announced. "Let's welcome our health teacher, Ms. Clementine. She has an empowering lesson to share. Please pay attention and be good listeners."

"Good morning, class," Ms. Clementine greeted the students. "Today we are going to learn about personal safety for your bodies. YOUR BODIES BELONG TO YOU. YOU CAN DECIDE WHO TOUCHES YOU."

"There are different kinds of touching," Ms. Clementine said. "Most touches are nice and make you feel good inside: like a kiss on the cheek, holding hands, and a cuddly hug. Can anyone else think of a good touch?"

Nora raised her hand first. "I like the way it feels to pet my animals," she answered.

"At the end of every soccer game," Peter added, "both teams line up and high-five each other."

Luci smiled and said, "I feel happy when my dad tucks me into bed at night."

"Terrific answers!" Ms. Clementine exclaimed.

"But sometimes a good touch might be confusing if it makes you feel uncomfortable," Ms. Clementine continued.

Rose shared, "When my uncle visits, he likes to give me a big hug. But I don't like it. I told my mom. She said, I don't have to hug my uncle anymore. Now when he visits, we just wave instead."

"Good example, Rose," Ms. Clementine responded. "If you don't like the way a hug feels, then you don't have to hug. I like the way you used your words."

"Always remember class, YOUR BODIES BELONG TO YOU. YOU CAN DECIDE WHO TOUCHES YOU."

Ms. Clementine went on. "Some touches are bad and can hurt. Being hit, kicked, and punched are examples of bad touches."

"Another type of bad touch that can hurt, or give you a bad feeling in your stomach, is if someone touches you on your private parts for no good reason. Your private parts are the parts of your body covered up when you wear your bathing suits. No one should see or touch your private parts, unless there is a good reason."

"Sometimes my dad helps me take a bath and get dressed," Jorge shared as a good reason.

"That's all right, Jorge," Ms. Clementine said. "In your own families and as long as you feel comfortable, that would be okay."

Luci raised her hand. "My mother said my doctor might have to see my private parts when I get a checkup."

"Yes, Luci," Ms. Clementine approved. "That would be a good reason as long as your mom or dad stay in the examination room with you."

"It is also important to know," Ms. Clementine added, "that it is WRONG if someone wants to take pictures of your private parts, or show you pictures of their private parts."

"This might give you a yucky and uncomfortable feeling in your stomach. Remember, private parts are private because we don't share them with other people, unless there is a good reason."

Ms. Clementine asked the students to find a seat on the rug in front of the whiteboard.

"In a few minutes," she said, "I'm going to teach you how to protect yourself from touches and feelings you don't like. But first, let's review some body part names."

"Here, you see a picture of a girl and boy wearing their bathing suits. Their private parts are covered up."

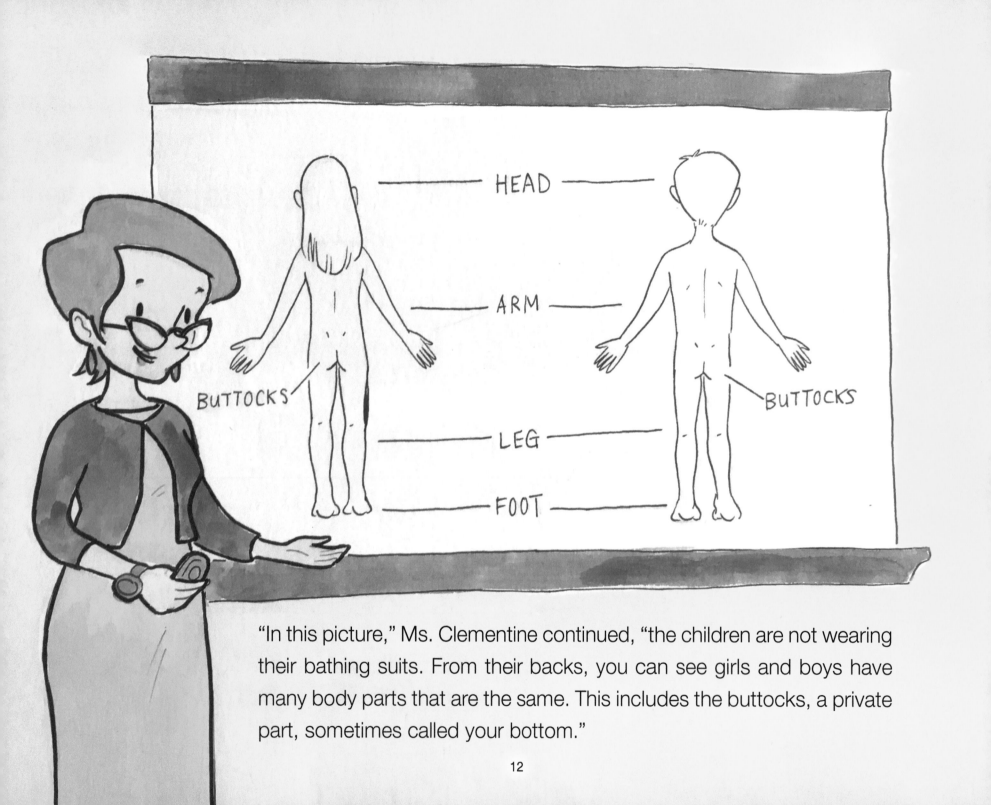

HEAD

ARM

BUTTOCKS

BUTTOCKS

LEG

FOOT

"In this picture," Ms. Clementine continued, "the children are not wearing their bathing suits. From their backs, you can see girls and boys have many body parts that are the same. This includes the buttocks, a private part, sometimes called your bottom."

Rose and Peter looked at each other and started to giggle.

Mr. Henry shared with the class, "Some people have nicknames and baby names for body parts. That's okay, but it is important to know the real names too."

Ms. Clementine advanced to the next picture, "From their fronts, you can see girls and boys have many body parts that are the same, but their private parts are different. Girls have breasts and a vagina. Boys have testicles and a penis."

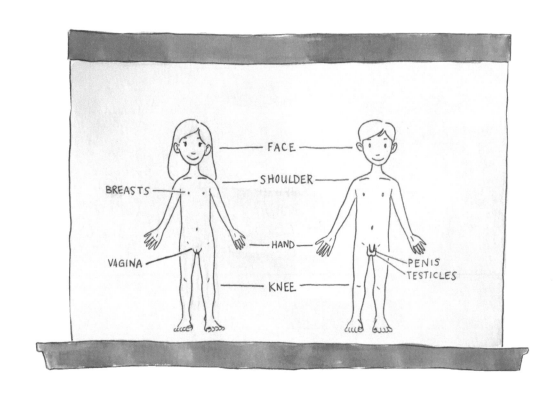

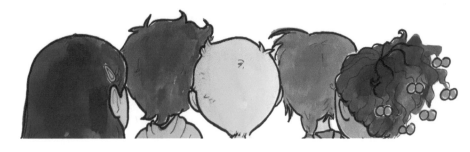

After reviewing the diagram, Ms. Clementine added, "I like the way everyone is being respectful and polite while we learn about personal safety."

"Now, class, listen carefully," Ms. Clementine explained, "because this is the MOST IMPORTANT part of today's lesson. You have the POWER to protect yourself from touches and feelings you don't like. All you have to do is remember three safety words. The first safety word is NO. Say, NO in a loud and clear voice if someone gives you a bad touch or a bad feeling."

NO

- No, I don't like that.
- No, don't do that again.
- No, don't touch me.
- No, stop it.
- No, I don't want to.

"The second safety word to remember is GO. If anyone is making you feel uncomfortable or hurting you, GO away from them as soon as you can."

GO

- Go away from the person hurting you.
- Go and leave if you can.
- Go to another room or location.
- Go to a place you feel safe.
- Go away if you feel uncomfortable.

Luci looked confused when she asked, "What if it's hard to say no, and you can't get away from the person giving you the bad touch or yucky feeling?"

"That is a good question, Luci," Ms. Clementine responded. "And the answer is why the last safety word is the MOST IMPORTANT WORD OF ALL!"

"Your third safety word is TELL! TELL a grown-up you trust what happened. TELL them about the bad touch or bad feeling. They will help you, and make sure it doesn't happen again."

"What if you TELL a grown-up about a bad touch and they don't believe you?" Jorge questioned.

"Oh, Jorge, that is a good point," Ms. Clementine emphasized. "If someone doesn't believe you, TELL another grown-up you trust and keep telling until someone does believe you."

"Could we TELL you?" Peter asked.

"Absolutely!" Ms. Clementine replied. "Because I would always believe you."

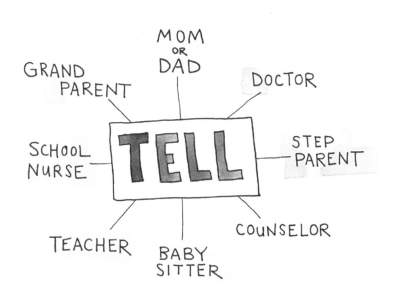

After Ms. Clementine introduced the third safety word, she asked the students if there were any other grown-ups they'd like to include on the TELL web. Jorge wanted to add aunts and uncles, and Rose said we should remember the recess monitors too. Everyone agreed.

Ms. Clementine advanced to the last picture to review.

"Always remember, class, YOUR BODIES BELONG TO YOU. YOU CAN DECIDE WHO TOUCHES YOU."

"If anyone ever gives you a bad touch or a bad feeling, remember your three safety words:

Say NO,
GO away, and
TELL a grown-up you trust."

20

Next, Ms. Clementine explained, "I am going to ask Mr. Henry to hand out a worksheet. While you answer your safety questions, I am going to sit at the back table. If anyone would like to talk to me, or ask me a question, please join me one at a time."

As the students got busy, Nora walked to the back of the room.

Nora stood across from Ms. Clementine and said in a quiet voice, "Last summer, I went on a family vacation. One afternoon when I was playing with my cousin, he gave me a bad touch. It made me feel embarrassed and uncomfortable."

"Oh, Nora," Ms. Clementine gently responded, "I am sorry this happened to you. But I want you to know, this was not your fault. You did not do anything wrong."

Then she asked, "Did you tell your parents?"

"No," Nora replied. "My cousin said in a mean voice, I better keep this a secret." Nora looked sad.

"Anytime a secret makes you feel bad, you must tell a grown-up," Ms. Clementine explained. "I am glad you told me Nora. After class, I am going to call your parents to let them know what happened to you. They will make sure this never happens again. I am very proud of you for telling me, and your parents will be very proud of you too!"

Nora looked relieved as she walked back to her desk.

Soon it was time for Ms. Clementine to leave the Lake Avenue School. Mr. Henry thanked her for visiting his classroom.

As Ms. Clementine started packing up, she announced, "I'm going to hand out an important letter for you to take home. It explains all the personal safety information you learned in today's lesson. Please share it with your parents and the grown-ups you live with."

Then she added, "Now, before I leave, I have one more question. Does anyone remember the three words that will give them the POWER to keep their body safe?"

The whole class smiled and shouted together, "NO, GO, and TELL!"

Ms. Clementine had the biggest smile of all.

Sample Copy of Letter to be Sent Home with Students After Personal Safety Lesson:

Dear Parents and Guardians,

Today I visited your child's classroom to teach a lesson on personal safety and sexual abuse prevention. I can assure you that prevention education is very successful in keeping children safe from sexual abuse and inappropriate touching, as well as helping your child disclose to someone they trust, if they have been a victim of abuse. This lesson is not meant to be a one time conversation, but rather a catalyst to start an ongoing discussion that will continue through adolescence and into adulthood.

I encourage you to talk with your child about:

1. Today's message: Your body belongs to you. You can decide who touches you.
2. Identifying good, bad, and uncomfortable touches and feelings.
3. Proper anatomical names for both male and female body parts.
4. Appropriate times for an adult to see or touch their private parts.
5. Ways to say NO to touches and feelings that are uncomfortable, confusing, or bad.
6. Safe places to GO if they find themselves in uncomfortable situations or being hurt.
7. Identifying grown-ups they can trust to TELL and talk to about feelings and touches.
8. Good and bad secrets and why we don't keep secrets that make them feel badly.
9. Recognizing threats and bribes that might be used to have them keep a secret.

10. Empowerment, in this regard: the process of becoming confident in controlling one's own body's rights concerning touches and feelings.

If your child makes a disclosure to you, it is imperative that you make sure your child is safe from harm and will not be subjected to this abuse again. Reassure your child that this was not his/her fault and that he/she did not do anything wrong. Seek counseling services for your child if you feel it is necessary. Report the abuse to the authorities, law enforcement, or contact your state's Child Protective Services. We must stop perpetrators from victimizing more children.

If a child makes a disclosure to an educational staff member in school, it becomes the school district's responsibility to make sure the child is safe, and will be returning home to a safe environment. If it is suspected that the child is being abused, Child Protective Services will need to be contacted. Please visit my web page, nogoandtell.com for more information and resources.

As adults, it is up to us to do everything possible to protect our children. Thank you for reinforcing personal safety prevention with your child.

Most sincerely,
Ms. Clementine
Family Life Educator
Lake Avenue School

Hotlines & Web Resources

The Childhelp National Child Abuse Hotline

800-4-A-CHILD (800-422-4453)

childhelp.org

RAINN

(Rape, Abuse, & Incest National Network)

800-656-HOPE (800-656-4673)

rainn.org

Darkness to Light

866-FOR-LIGHT (866-367-5444)

darkness2light.org

For more information and resources for parents and educators visit:

nogoandtell.com

About the Author

Marilyn A. Pittelli began her thirty-six year teaching career after receiving both her bachelor's and master's degrees in health education. During this time, she held the title of Family Life Educator for the Saratoga Springs City School District in New York State. In this position, Ms. Pittelli's primary responsibility was to teach sexual abuse prevention to every student from kindergarten to sixth grade. She was also instrumental in revising and rewriting the district's family life curriculum which she implemented to over three thousand students each year. Her experience and expertise in prevention education allowed her to develop a very successful program designed to keep children safe from sexual abuse, as well as provide children who have been abused with the language they need to make a disclosure to a trusted adult.

Marilyn A. Pittelli is passionate about preventing every child from becoming a victim of sexual abuse. Determined to make a difference, she wrote, *NO, GO, AND TELL! Ms. Clementine's Personal Safety Lesson* to provide parents and educators with the resources and skills to teach personal safety to all children in a comfortable and safe environment.